Air Fryer Cookbook for Beginners

Hassle-Free Recipes for Beginners and Advanced Cooks.

Fry, Bake, Grill, and Roast Healthy Meal at Home

Mary Carton

Copyright © 2020 by Mary Carton

Legal Disclaimer

The information contained in this book and its contents is not designed to replace any form of medical or professional advice; and is not meant to replace the need for independent medical, financial, legal, or other professional advice or services that may be required. The content and information in this book have been provided for educational and entertainment purposes only.

The content and information contained in this book have been compiled from sources deemed reliable, and they are accurate to the best of the Author's knowledge, information, and belief. However, the Author cannot guarantee its accuracy and validity and therefore cannot be held liable for any errors and/or omissions. Further, changes are periodically made to this book as needed. Where appropriate and/or necessary, you must consult a professional (including but not limited to your doctor, attorney, financial advisor, or other such professional) before using any of the suggested remedies, techniques, and/or information in this book.

Upon using this book's contents and information, you agree to hold harmless the Author from any damages, costs, and expenses, including any legal fees potentially resulting from the application of any of the information in this book. This disclaimer applies to any loss, damages, or injury caused by the use and application of this book's contents, whether directly or indirectly, whether for breach of contract, tort, negligence, personal injury, criminal intent, or under any other circumstance.

Table of Contents

The Basics of Air Fryer

Before diving deep into the recipes themselves, I think we must have an understanding of the individual appliances that we are working with here. Since this book has a vast compilation of 900+ recipes that span a multitude of appliances, having a good understanding of each of them will help you get the best out of each of the recipes!

That being said, let's start with the most question first,

What is an Air Fryer?

To keep things short and straightforward, Air Fryer is one of the most unique and innovative appliances to hit the market!

This is an excellent cooking appliance that utilizes the power of superheated "Air" and carefully placed exhaust fans to evenly distribute hot air around the food and perfectly cook the meal, with minimal oil usage!

Upon its release, the Air Fryer broke some boundaries and became an instant hit. It's popularity reached such levels that even Gordon Ramsay took notice and claimed that "Air Is The New Oil."

The cooking mechanism of the device is what makes it so "Unique."

While other kitchen appliances tend to rely on the technique of conduction mostly, Air Fryers differentiate themselves from the crow by implementing the flow of air into the cooking process and cook the meals through the method of "Convection."

Using Air, and the so-called "Rapid Air Technology," which I have talked about in the next section.

Having a look at how the Air Fry works

Now that you have a good idea of what the Air Fryer is let me briefly breakdown how the Air Fryer works.

Well, it's pretty simple if you think about it.

The keyword here is "Air."

Most other conventional cooking appliances tend to cook their meal by using some sort of heater that passes heat through the meal through a process known as conduction. This transfers heat to the meal in touch.

An Air Fryer, on the other hand, does its cooking through a process called "Convection," where the air is heated up and circulated throughout the food.

During your journey into the various supermarkets looking for an Air Fryer, you have most definitely seen the word "Rapid Air Technology" countless times. That refers to a very delicately designed process that the Air Fryer uses to cook its food.

The Air has sucked up the intake chamber, and the appliance gets heated up.

Cleaning And Maintenance

The longevity of your appliance largely depends on how you take care of the appliance itself in the long run. Over time, dirt and debris might accumulate on the various parts of the appliance. You must keep your Air Fryer in tip shape to ensure that it can provide you with the best performance and output possible.

While cleaning your device, you should follow the following steps for maximum efficiency!

- Make sure to remove the power cable from the outlet
- Wipe the external part of the fryer using a moist cloth dipped in mild detergent
- Clean the cooking basket and Fryer Tray with hot water and a soft sponge (dipped in mild detergent)
- Clean the inner parts using hot water and soft sponge (similarly dipped in mild detergent)
- Brush the heating element carefully to clear out any stuck residue

Amazing advantages of the Air Fryer

With all of that being said, there are many reasons as to why you should buy an Air Fryer! Below are just some of the amazing benefits that you might expect while using the Air Fryer!

- The Air Fryer is an extremely versatile appliance that will allow you to not only Air Fry dishes but also grill, roast, or even bake them as well!

- The enclosure of the Air Fryer is constructed keeping the safety of its users as the top priority, and it eliminates the risk of having hot oil falling over your skin

- The appliance is extremely easy and simple to use. The minimal use of oil results in very little built of debris/grease, which is very seamless to clean as well

- The pre-installed smart programs of the appliance are very carefully designed to help even amateur chefs prepare premium quality dishes

- Since you are cooking with superheated air here, the Air Fryer helps to save a lot of time, freeing up more of your day to spend with the people you love, and doing the things that you love

- Using the Air Fryer cuts down almost 8-85% of total oil consumption, which makes it great for your heart in the long run

- The relatively compact size and versatility of the Air Fryer means that you can easily install it in any corner of your kitchen (given it gets proper airflow) and free up space to keep your kitchen sleek and clean looking

And those are just the tip of the iceberg!

General cooking timetable

While this book already has the required temperature specified in all of the recipes, it is still important to know the general cooking temperatures of different ingredients, as it will help you significantly when trying to come up with your very own masterpieces!

Meat

	Cooking Temperature (Fahrenheit)	Cooking Time (Minutes)
Bacon	350	8-12
Chicken (Whole)	350	45-65
Chicken Breasts (Bone-In)	375	25-35
Chicken Breasts (Boneless)	350	15-20
Chicken Tenders	350	8-12
Chicken Thighs (Bone-In)	400	15-22
Chicken Thighs (Boneless)	375	16-21
Chicken Wings	375	18-28
Lamb (Leg)	375	18-28
Lamb (Rack)	375	10-17
NY Strip Steak	400	8-14
Pork Chops	350	10-15
Pork Tenderloin	375	15-25
Ribeye/T-Bone	400	15-25

Ground Meat

	Cooking Temperature (Fahrenheit)	Cooking Time (Minutes)
Burger Patties (1/4 lb)	350	8-15
Meatballs	375	6-9
Sausages (raw)	375	15-20
Sausages (cooked)	375	7-12

Chopped Sea/Food

	Cooking Temperature (Fahrenheit)	Cooking Time (Minutes)
Chicken	400	8-15
Pork	375	8-12
Steak	400	8-12
Salmon	400	6-12
Tilapia	350	6-10

Others

	Cooking Temperature (Fahrenheit)	Cooking Time (Minutes)
Banana, sliced	375	6-8
Chickpeas	400	12-17
Tofu, cubed	375	12-17
Tortilla chips	350	3-8
Pizza, personal size	375	7-12

Frozen Food

	Cooking Temperature (Fahrenheit)	Cooking Time (Minutes)
Chicken Tenders, breaded and pre-cooked	375	14-18
Dumplings/Potstickers	400	6-10
Egg Rolls	350	8-14
Fish Sticks	400	8-12
French Fries	400	14-17
Hash Browns	325	6-9
Mini Pizzas	375	8-15
Mozzarella Sticks	375	7-10
Onion Rings	400	8-10
Tater Tots	400	10-15

Vegetables

	Cooking Temperature (Fahrenheit)	Cooking Time (Minutes)
Broccoli	400	5-9
Brussels Sprouts, halved	375	9-16
Butternut Squash, chopped	400	15-20
Carrots, chopped	400	10-15
Cauliflower, whole	350	15-20
Cauliflower, chopped	400	10-15
Corn on the Cob	400	8-10
Eggplant	400	15-18
Green Beans	400	8-10
Kale Leaves	375	4-5
Mushrooms, Button	375	8-13
Mushrooms, Portobellos	350	10-12
Okra	350	12-14
Onions, sliced	400	8-10
Parsnips, chopped	375	10-16
Peppers, small	400	4-8
Potatoes, whole	400	30-45
Potatoes, chopped	375	15-30
Sweet Potatoes, chopped	400	8-15
Sweet Potatoes, whole	375	30-245
Tomatoes, cherry	350	5-8
Tomatoes, halved	350	6-12
Zucchini, chopped	350	8-12
Zucchini, noodles	400	10-20

Recipes

Creamy Mustard Air Chicken

Serving: 4

Prep Time: 20 minutes

Cook Time: 50 minutes

Ingredients:

- 4 garlic cloves
- 8 chicken slices
- 1 tablespoon thyme leaves
- ½ cup dry wine vinegar
- Salt as needed
- ½ cup Dijon mustard
- 2 cups almond meal
- 2 tablespoons melted butter
- 1 tablespoon lemon zest
- 2 tablespoons olive oil

Directions:

1. Pre-heat your Air Fryer to 350 degrees F

2. Take a bowl and add garlic, salt, cloves, almond meal, pepper, olive oil, melted butter, and lemon zest

3. Take another bowl and mix mustard and wine

4. Place chicken slices in the wine mixture and then in the crumb mixture

5. Transfer prepared chicken to your Air Fryer cooking basket and cook for 40 minutes.

6. Serve and enjoy!

Nutritional Contents:

- Calories: 762
- Fat: 24g
- Carbohydrates: 3g
- Protein: 76g

Breaded Chicken Cutlets

Serving: 4

Prep Time: 20 minutes

Cook Time: 25 minutes

Ingredients:

- ¼ cup parmesan
- 4 chicken breasts
- 1/8 teaspoon paprika
- ¼ teaspoon pepper
- 2 tablespoons panko breadcrumbs
- 1 teaspoons parsley
- ½ teaspoon garlic powder
- 1 bread loaf

Directions:

1. Pre-heat your Air Fryer to 400 degrees F.
2. Take a bowl and mix in parmesan and panko.
3. Mix in garlic powder, pepper, paprika.
4. Mix well.
5. Wash and cut your chicken breasts.

6. Take a bowl and add water, take another bowl and add bread to the bowl. Gently mash it.

7. Cover chicken with panko mix and form chicken cutlets.

8. Add bread to your chicken cutlet and transfer cutlets to Air Fryer.

9. Cook for 25 minutes.

10. Serve and enjoy!

Nutritional Contents:

- Calories: 270
- Fat: 13g
- Carbohydrates: 17g
- Protein: 36g

Chicken BBQ Satay

Serving: 4

Prep Time: 10 minutes

Cook Time: 10 minutes

Ingredients:

- ¾ ounces boneless and skinless chicken tenders
- ½ cup low-sodium soy sauce
- ½ cup pineapple juice
- ¼ cup sesame oil
- 4 cloves garlic, chopped
- 1 tablespoon fresh ginger, grated
- 4 scallions, chopped
- 2 teaspoons toasted sesame seeds
- 1 pinch of black pepper

Directions:

1. Skewer the chicken pieces into the skewers and trim any fat.

2. Take a large-sized bowl and add the remaining ingredients.

3. Dip the skewered chicken into the seasoning bowl.

4. Pre-heat your Air Fryer to 390 degrees Fahrenheit.

5. Remove the chicken and place them on a towel to dry them.

6. Remove the chicken and cook for 5-7 minutes.

7. Have fun!

Nutritional Contents:

- Calories: 361
- Fat: 12g
- Carbohydrates: 37g
- Protein: 26g

Buttermilk Chicken

Serving: 4

Prep Time: 20 minutes

Cook Time: 20 minutes

Ingredients:

- 6 chicken thigh, skin on and bone-in
- 2 cups buttermilk
- 2 teaspoon salt
- 2 teaspoons black pepper
- 1 teaspoon cayenne pepper
- 2 cups all-purpose flour
- 1 tablespoon baking powder
- 1 tablespoon garlic powder
- 1 tablespoon paprika
- 1 tablespoon salt

Directions:

1. Rinse the chicken well and pat them dry, making sure to remove any fat residue.

2. Pat them dry.

3. Take a large-sized bowl and add paprika, black pepper, and salt alongside the chicken.

4. Toss them well.

5. Pour buttermilk over the chicken and coat them well.

6. Allow them to chill overnight.

7. Pre-heat your Air Fryer to 400 degrees F.

8. Take a bowl and add flour, paprika, pepper, and salt.

9. Coat the chicken with the flour mix.

10. Place them in a single layer in the Air Fryer basket and cook for 10 minutes.

11. Keep repeating until the chicken is cooked.

12. Enjoy!

Nutritional Contents:

- Calories: 422
- Fat: 27g
- Carbohydrates: 8g
- Protein: 3g

Whole Freestyle Chicken

Serving: 4

Prep Time: 30 minutes

Cooking Time: 1 hour

Ingredients:

- 1 whole chicken
- Poultry seasoning
- Olive oil

Directions:

1. Remove the giblet packet from the chicken
2. Pat the chicken fry
3. Preheat your Air Fryer to 350 degrees F
4. Put olive oil on the chicken
5. Place the chicken in the Air Fryer
6. Cook for 30 minutes
7. Flip the chicken and then cook for half an hour more
8. Let it cool for 15 minutes
9. Serve and enjoy!

Nutritional Contents:

- Calories: 167.7
- Fat: 6.6g
- Carbohydrates: 4g
- Protein: 25g

Grilled Hawaiian Chicken

Serving: 2

Prep Time: 10 minutes

Cook Time: 15 minutes

Ingredients:

- 4 chicken breasts
- 2 garlic clove
- ½ cup ketchup, Keto-friendly
- ½ teaspoon ginger
- ½ cup coconut aminos
- 2 tablespoons red wine vinegar
- ½ cup pineapple juice
- 2 tablespoons apple cider vinegar

Directions:

1. Pre-heat your Air Fryer to 360 degrees F.
2. Take a bowl and mix in ketchup, pineapple juice, cider vinegar, ginger.
3. Take frying and place it over low heat, add sauce, and let it heat up.

4. Cover chicken with the aminos and vinegar pour hot sauce on top.

5. Let the chicken sit for 15 minutes to marinade.

6. Transfer chicken to your Air Fryer and bake for 15 minutes.

7. Serve and enjoy!

Nutritional Contents:

- Calories: 200
- Fat: 3g
- Carbohydrates: 10g
- Protein: 29g

Turmeric Chicken Liver

Serving: 5

Prep Time: 10 minutes

Cooking Time: 10 minutes

Ingredients:

- 17-ounce chicken liver
- 2 tablespoons almond flour
- 1 tablespoon coconut oil
- ½ teaspoon salt
- ¼ teaspoon garlic, minced
- ¾ cup chicken stock

Directions:

1. Pre-heat your Air Fryer to 400 degrees F

2. Add coconut oil to Air Fryer cooking basket and pre-heat for 20 seconds

3. Stir well and cook for 2 minutes at 400 degrees F

4. Sprinkle chicken liver with almond flour, salt, and minced garlic

5. Add chicken stock, stir liver and cook for 5 minutes

6. Serve meat and enjoy it!

Nutritional Contents:

- Calories: 250
- Fat: 26g
- Carbohydrates: 3g
- Protein: 35g

Healthy Air Fried Chicken Meatballs

Serving: 7

Prep Time: 20 minutes

Cooking Time: 10 to 12 minutes

Ingredients:

- 2 green onions, finely chopped
- 1 pound of ground chicken
- 1 tablespoon soy sauce
- 1 tablespoon Hoisin sauce
- ½ cup cilantro, chopped
- 1 teaspoon sesame oil
- 1 teaspoon Sriracha
- ¼ cup coconut, unsweetened shredded
- 1 pinch ground black pepper
- 1 pinch salt

Directions:

1. Preheat your Air Fryer at 350 F
2. Take a large bowl and mix all the ingredients into it
3. Then take a paper sheet and line Air Fryer
4. Put the baking pan in your Air Fryer and lock it
5. Cook for 10 to 12 minutes at 380 F

6. Once cooked, let it cool for 5 minutes

7. Serve and enjoy!

Nutritional Contents:

- Calories: 218
- Fat: 8g
- Carbohydrates: 7g
- Protein: 30g

Asiago Chicken

Serving: 4

Prep Time: 5 minutes

Cook Time: 45 minutes

Ingredients:

- 4 chicken breasts
- 1 teaspoon garlic powder
- 1 cup mayonnaise
- ½ teaspoon pepper
- ½ cup soft cheese
- ½ teaspoon salt
- Chopped basil for garnish

Directions:

1. Pre-heat your Air Fryer to 380 degrees F.
2. Take a bowl and add cheese, mayonnaise garlic, powder and salt, and mix to make a marinade.
3. Cover your chicken with the marinade.

4. Transfer chicken to your Air Fryer and cook for 45 minutes.

5. Serve with a garnish of chopped basil.

Nutritional Contents:

- Calories: 250
- Fat: 6g
- Carbohydrates: 33g
- Protein: 14g

KFC Chicken Tenders

Serving: 4

Prep Time: 10 minutes

Cook Time: 15 minutes

Ingredients:

- ¾ pound chicken tenders

For Breading

- 2 whole eggs, beaten
- ½ cup seasoned breadcrumbs
- ½ cup all-purpose flour
- 1 teaspoon black pepper
- 2 tablespoons olive oil

Directions:

1. Pre-heat your Fryer to 330 degrees F.

2. Take three bowls and add breadcrumbs, eggs, and flour individually.

3. Season the breadcrumbs with salt and pepper.

4. Add olive oil to the breadcrumbs and mix well.

5. Dredge the chicken tenders into the flour, eggs, and finally, In the bread crumbs.

6. Take out your crumb covered tendered and place them in your Air Fryer cooking basket.

7. Cook for 10 minutes.

8. Increase the temperature to 390 degrees F and cook for 5 minutes more.

9. Enjoy!

Nutritional Contents:

- Calories: 400
- Fat: 5g
- Carbohydrates: 20g
- Protein: 88g

Chicken And Prawn Paste

Serving: 3

Prep Time: 10 minutes

Cook Time: 20 minutes

Ingredients:

- 8 chicken wings
- ½ teaspoon sugar
- 2 tablespoons cornflour
- ½ tablespoon wine
- 1 tablespoon shrimp paste
- 1 teaspoon ginger
- 1/ teaspoon olive oil

Directions:

1. Pre-heat your Air Fryer to 360 degrees F.

2. Wash your chicken wings thoroughly and cut it.

3. Take a bowl and add olive oil, ginger, wine, and sugar.

4. Cover the chicken wings with the prepared marinade.

5. Cover chicken with flour.

6. Cover the floured chicken with shrimp paste.

7. Transfer prepared chicken to your Air Fryer and bake for 20 minutes.

8. Serve and enjoy!

Nutritional Contents:

- Calories: 110
- Fat: 5g
- Carbohydrates: 7g
- Protein: 7g

Chicken Enchiladas

Serving: 6

Prep Time: 25 minutes

Cook Time: 60 minutes

Ingredients:

- 3 cups chicken
- 2 cups cheese
- ½ cup of salsa
- 1 can green chilies
- 12 flour tortillas
- 2 cans enchilada sauce

Directions:

1. Pre-heat your Fryer to 400 degrees F.
2. Take a bowl and mix salsa and enchilada sauce and sauce.
3. Mix in chopped chicken.
4. Transfer the chicken from the sauce to the tortillas and roll the tortillas up.
5. Top tortillas with cheese and bake in your Air Fryer for 60 minutes.
6. Serve and enjoy!

Nutritional Contents:

- Calories: 226
- Fat: 14g
- Carbohydrates: 13g
- Protein: 16g

Honey And Orange Chicken

Serving: 4

Prep Time: 30 minutes

Cook Time: 30 minutes

Ingredients:

- 1 and ½ pounds of chicken breast
- Parsley to taste
- 1 cup coconut
- ¼ cup of coconut oil
- ¾ cup breadcrumbs
- 2 whole eggs
- ½ cup flour
- ½ teaspoon pepper
- Salt to taste1/2 cup orange marmalade
- 1 teaspoon red pepper flakes
- ¼ cup honey
- 3 tablespoons Dijon mustard

Directions:

1. Pre-heat your Air Fryer to 400 degrees F.

2. Wash your chicken thoroughly and cut it into slices.

3. Take a bowl and blend in coconut, breadcrumbs, flour, salt, parsley, and pepper.

4. Take another plate and add eggs.

5. Take a frying pan and place it over medium heat, add coconut oil, and let it heat up.

6. Dredge the chicken in egg mix, flour, and then with panko.

7. Transfer prepared chicken to your Air Fryer and bake for 15 minutes.

8. Take a bowl and mix in honey, marmalade, mustard, and pepper flakes.

9. Cover chicken with marmalade mix and cook for 5 minutes more.

10. Serve and enjoy!

Nutritional Contents:

- Calories: 246
- Fat: 6g
- Carbohydrates: 21g
- Protein: 25g

Hot Air Fryer Kabobs

Serving: 2

Prep Time: 3 minutes

Cook Time: 15 minutes

Ingredients:

- 1 chicken breast
- 2 lemon, juiced and rind reserved
- 1 tablespoon chicken seasoning
- 1 teaspoon garlic puree
- Handful of peppercorns
- Salt and pepper to taste

Directions:

1. Preheat your Air Fryer to 352 degrees F.

2. Take a large-sized sheet of silver foil and work on top, add all of the seasonings alongside the lemon rind.

3. Layout the chicken breast onto a chopping board and trim any fat and little bones.

4. Season each side with the pepper and salt.

5. Rub the chicken seasoning on both sides well.

6. Place on your silver foil sheet and rub.

7. Seal it up tightly.

8. Slap it with a rolling pin and flatten it.

9. Place it in your Air Fryer and cook for 15 minutes until the center is fully cooked.

10. Serve and enjoy!

Nutritional Contents:

- Calories: 301
- Fat: 22g
- Carbohydrates: 11
- Protein: 23g

Air Fryer Chicken Kabobs

Serving: 3

Prep Time: 30 minutes

Cooking Time: 20 minutes

Ingredients:

- 6 mushrooms chop in half
- 3 chicken breasts, diced
- 3 bell peppers, take 3 different colors to look good
- Sesame
- 1/3 cup honey
- 1/3 cup soy sauce
- Oil a few sprays
- Salt
- pepper

Directions:

1. Cut 3 chicken breasts into cubes

2. Add a pinch of pepper, oil, and salt

3. Add honey and soy sauce, then mix

4. Then put some sesame seeds and stir well

5. Arrange peppers, mushroom pieces, and chicken into the skewers

6. Preheat your Air Fryer to 340 degrees F

7. Coat the chicken kabobs with mixed sauce

8. Place all the chicken kabobs in the Air Fryer basket

9. Cook for 20 minutes

10. Serve and enjoy!

Nutritional Contents:

- Calories: 288
- Fat: 3.5g
- Carbohydrates: 6.5g
- Protein: 55.9g

Sesame Chicken Meal

Serving: 3

Prep Time: 15 minutes

Cook Time: 30 minutes

Ingredients:

- Sesame oil as needed
- Salt and pepper to taste
- 1 teaspoon oregano
- 1 garlic clove, minced
- 1 drizzle of olive oil
- ½ lemon, juiced
- 1 chicken breast, cut in half

Directions:

1. Pre-heat your Vortex Air Fryer to 360 degrees F

2. Take a pan and place it over medium heat, add oil and let it heat up

3. Add spices, garlic, lemon, oil and stir gently until garlic is slightly brown

4. Add chicken breast and gently coat

5. Transfer to the cooking basket and cook for 30 minutes or until golden

6. Serve and enjoy!

Nutritional Contents:

- Calories: 581
- Fat: 30g
- Carbohydrates: 57g
- Protein: 24g

Herby Chicken Wings

Serving: 4

Prep Time: 15 minutes

Cook Time: 40 minutes

Ingredients:

- 2¼ pounds wing sticks
- Salt to taste Oregano to taste
- Black pepper to taste
- Garlic to taste Grated onion to taste
- Lemon to taste Olive oil

Directions:

1. Pre-heat your Vortex Air Fryer to 400 degrees F

2. Season the drumsticks, with the previous elements, marinate for about 15 min.

3. Pour oil over the drumsticks and stir well, spreading the oil over all of them.

4. Transfer to the cooking basket, cook for 30-40 minutes until golden

5. Serve and enjoy!

Nutritional Contents:

- Calories: 200
- Fat: 3g
- Carbohydrates: 3g
- Protein: 17g

Roast White Wing Turkey

Serving: 4-6

Prep Time: 30 minutes

Cook Time: 4 hours

Ingredients:

- 1 turkey
- ½ cup vinegar
- ½ bottle dry white wine
- 1 lemon, juiced
- 2 teaspoons red pepper sauce
- 1 tablespoon salt
- 1 onion
- 3 garlic cloves
- 1 bay leaf
- ½ pound mayonnaise
- ½ potatoes, browned

Directions:

1. Preheat your Air Fryer to 360 degrees F

2. Wash the turkey thoroughly and rain

3. Take a bowl and mix in spices, mayonnaise and rub inside and outside of the turkey

4. Transfer to your Fryer and bake for about 4 hours, covering it with an aluminum foil

5. Remove once done

6. Serve with potatoes, browned potatoes, and enjoy!

Nutritional Contents:

- Calories: 214
- Fat: 8g
- Carbohydrates: 0.1g
- Protein: 32g

Simple Roasted Turkey Breast

Serving: 4

Prep Time: 20 minutes

Cook Time: 30 minutes

Ingredients:

- 1 and ¼ pound boneless turkey breast
- 1 cup orange broth
- ½ can guaran diet salt
- Garlic and vinegar as needed

Directions:

1. Preheat your Air Fryer to 360 degrees F

2. Season turkey with garlic, salt, and pepper

3. Add orange juice and salt, let the turkey soak in the mix for 2 hours

4. Transfer to Fryer to 30 minutes

5. Serve and enjoy!

Nutritional Contents:

- Calories: 152
- Fat: 0.8g
- Carbohydrates: 0g
- Protein: 34g

Delicious Turkey Fillet

Serving: 4

Prep Time: 60 minutes

Cook Time: 30 minutes

Ingredients:

- 1 pound turkey fillets
- 1 package of cream
- 1 can of rolled mushrooms
- 3 onions
- 1 glass of wine
- Enough olive oil
- Enough Black lemon pepper to taste
- Salt to taste

Directions:

1. Preheat your Air Fryer to 400 degrees F
2. Take your fillets and cut them into thin strips, the season for 1 hour with lemon juice, salt, and pepper
3. Take a frying pan and add oil, let it heat up and add onion slices, pour olive oil and cook until brown, remove them
4. Transfer fillets to your cooking basket and cook for 30 minutes
5. Add mushrooms and wine to the frying pan, cook until reduced, and the mushrooms are cooked
6. Add onion to the frying pan and top with cream, bring the mix to a boil
7. Season and pour the mix over fillets
8. Serve and enjoy!

Nutritional Contents:

- Calories: 156
- Fat: 1g
- Carbohydrates: 0g
- Protein: 35g

Flavorful Turkey Breast

Serving: 4

Prep Time: 20 minutes

Cook Time: 50 minutes

Ingredients:

- 1 pound smoked turkey breast
- 1 tablespoon butter
- 2 cups dry white wine
- 2 tablespoons honey
- 1 teaspoon flour
- 3 stalks green onions, chopped

Directions:

1. Pre-heat your Vortex Air Fryer to 360 degrees F

2. Cut the turkey breast into thick slices, about 1 cm thick. Remove the outer layer that surrounds the meat with a sharp knife.

3. Brown turkey breast slices on both sides in the air fryer at 360 F for 20 minutes.

4. Remove and arrange the slices on the serving plate, keeping it in a warm place.

5. Heat the wine. When it boils, add the honey, previously mixing it with the flour.

6. Stir with a spatula until you have a slightly thick sauce.

7. Add the green onions and then pour, little by little, over the heated turkey slices.

Nutritional Contents:

- Calories: 156
- Fat: 1g
- Carbohydrates: 0g
- Protein: 35g

Hawaiian Stuffed Quail

Serving: 4

Prep Time: 20 minutes

Cook Time: 20-30 minutes

Ingredients:

- 1 cup champagne
- 1 cup of water
- ½ tablespoon ground pepper
- 2 teaspoon salt
- 3 teaspoon curry
- 3 teaspoon virgin olive oil
- 3 garlic cloves, minced
- 3 and ½ teaspoon lemon vinegar
- 4 medium-sized Hawaiian pineapples
- 4 quail, cleaned and washed
- 20 slices endive leaves

Directions:

1. Cut the pineapple curry slices. Reserve.
2. Heat 2 tablespoons of oil in a frying pan and brown the pineapple slices on both sides.

3. Chop them and fill the quail. Tie well Place on the baking sheet—season with champagne, water, salt, and garlic.
4. Bake in the air fryer for 40 minutes or until golden brown.
5. Arrange the quail on the plates. Add endive and reserve.
6. Mix the vinegar, remaining oil, and pepper—endive water. Pineapple, rosemary, and thyme leave to decorate.

Nutritional Contents:

- Calories: 246
- Fat: 16g
- Carbohydrates: 1g
- Protein: 23g

Feisty Wrapped Duck

Serving: 4

Prep Time: 20 minutes

Cook Time: 90 minutes

Ingredients:

- 1 pound duck, 3 pounds
- 1 and ½ tablespoons butter
- 1 sprig rosemary
- Salt and pepper to taste
- Wine as needed

Directions:

1. Pre-heat your Vortex Air Fryer to 400 degrees F

2. Season duck inside out with salt and pepper, add sage, rosemary inside and sew carefully to keep the shape

3. Wrap duck with to a sheet of parchment paper, greased with butter, wrap with aluminum foil over that

4. Transfer to Air Fryer cooking basket and cook for 90 minutes

5. Serve and enjoy!

Nutritional Contents:

- Calories: 119
- Fat: 2g
- Carbohydrates: 0g
- Protein: 2g

The Creamy Quail

Serving: 4

Prep Time: 10 minutes

Cook Time: 20 minutes

Ingredients:

- 2 and ¼ pounds quail
- 3 tablespoons margarine
- 2 tablespoons olive oil
- 1 large onion, grated
- 2 tablespoons wheat flour
- 1 cup white wine
- 1 can sour cream
- 5 and ¼ ounces mozzarella cut into cubes

Directions:

1. Preheat your Air Fryer to 360 degrees F

2. Take a boiling pot and add quail, boil for 5 minutes

3. Take a pan and add oil, place it over medium heat, add oil and let it heat up

4. Add onion, Sauté until golden

5. Add flour, mix well with a spoon until golden

6. Add wine and boil until reduced

7. Add mozzarella

8. Add cream, salt, pepper, and wait until the mix boils

9. Remove heat

10. Transfer quail to your cooking basket and pour the sauce on top

11. Add more parmesan

12. Bake for 20 minutes until golden

13. Serve and enjoy!

Nutritional Contents:

- Calories: 246
- Fat: 1g
- Carbohydrates: 16g
- Protein: 23g

Simple Grilled Fish And Cheese

Serving: 4

Prep Time: 5 minutes

Cooking Time: 7 minutes

Ingredients:

- 1 bunch basil
- 2 garlic cloves
- 1 tablespoon olive oil (for cooking)
- ¼ cup olive oil (extra)
- 1 tablespoon parmesan cheese
- Salt and pepper to taste
- 2 tablespoons Pinenuts
- 6 ounces white fish fillet

Directions:

1. Brush the fish fillets with oil and season with some pepper and salt

2. Pre-heat your Air Fryer to a temperature of 356 degrees Fahrenheit

3. Carefully transfer the fillets to your Air Fryer cooking basket

4. Cook for about 8 minutes

5. Take a small bowl and add basil, olive oil, pine nuts, garlic, parmesan cheese and blend using your hand

6. Serve this mixture with the fish!

Nutritional Contents:

- Calories: 344
- Fat: 26g
- Carbohydrates: 7g
- Protein: 21g

Dill Sauce And Salmon

Serving: 4

Prep Time: 10 minutes

Cooking Time: 35 minutes

Ingredients:

Salmon

- 4 salmon, each of 6 ounces
- 2 teaspoons olive oil
- 1 pinch salt

Dill Sauce

- ½ cup non-fat Greek yogurt
- ½ cup sour cream
- Pinch of salt
- 2 tablespoons chopped dill

Directions:

1. Pre-heat your Air Fryer to 270 degrees F
2. Drizzle cut pieces of salmon with 1 teaspoon olive oil
3. Season with salt
4. Take the cooking basket out and transfer salmon to basket, cook for 20-23 minutes

5. Take a bowl and add sour cream, salt, chopped dill, yogurt and mix well to prepare the dill sauce

6. Serve cooked salmon by pouring the sauce all over

7. Garnish with chopped dill and enjoy!

Nutritional Contents:

- Calories: 696
- Fat: 45g
- Carbohydrates: 2g
- Protein: 62g

Awesome Cajun Shrimp

Serving: 4

Prep Time: 5 minutes

Cooking Time: 7 minutes

Ingredients:

- 1 and ¼ pound tiger shrimp, about 16-20 pieces
- ¼ teaspoon cayenne pepper
- ½ teaspoon old bay seasoning
- ¼ teaspoon smoked paprika
- 1 pinch of salt
- 1 tablespoon olive oil

Directions:

1. Pre-heat your Air Fryer to 390 degrees F

2. Take a mixing bowl and add Ingredients: (except shrimp), mix well

3. Dip the shrimp into spice mixture and oil

4. Transfer the prepared shrimp to your cooking basket and cook for 5 minutes

5. Serve and enjoy!

Nutritional Contents:

- Calories: 176
- Fat: 2g
- Carbohydrates: 5g
- Protein: 23g

Fresh Broiled Tilapia

Serving: 4

Prep Time: 5 minutes

Cook Time: 10 minutes

Ingredients:

- 1 pound tilapia fillets
- Old bay seasoning as needed
- Canola oil as needed
- Lemon pepper as needed
- Salt to taste
- Butter buds

Directions:

1. Pre-heat your Air Fryer to 400 degrees F.
2. Cover tilapia with oil.
3. Take a bowl and mix in salt, lemon pepper, butter buds, seasoning.
4. Cover your fish with the sauce.
5. Bake fillets for 10 minutes.
6. Serve and enjoy!

Nutritional Contents:

- Calories: 177
- Fat: 10g
- Carbohydrates: 1.2g
- Protein: 25g

Cheesy Bacon Wrapped Shrimp

Serving: 4

Prep Time: 20 minutes

Cooking Time: 6 minutes

Ingredients:

- 16 extra-large raw shrimp, peeled, deveined and butterflied
- The ¼ cup BBQ sauce
- 16 slices of bacon, cooked halfway
- 16 cubes cheddar jack cheese

Directions:

1. Preheat your Air Fryer to 350 degrees F

2. Fill shrimp with a cheese cube and wrap with a slice of bacon

3. Use a toothpick to secure the bacon to the shrimp

4. Brush them with BBQ sauce

5. Place them in the Air Fryer and cook for 6 minutes

6. Serve and enjoy!

Nutritional Contents:

- Calories: 235
- Fat: 9g
- Carbohydrates: 4g
- Protein: 32g

Fish Lettuce Wraps

Serving: 3

Prep Time: 20 minutes

Cooking Time: 10 minutes

Ingredients:

- 6 small fillets of tilapia
- 6 iceberg lettuce leaves
- ½ cup carrot, shredded
- ½ teaspoon black pepper, ground
- 2 teaspoons Cajun seasoning
- 1 teaspoon salt
- 1 tablespoon olive oil
- 1 tablespoon lemon juice
- ½ cup purple cabbage, shredded

Directions:

1. Preheat your Air Fryer to 390 degrees F
2. Season tilapia with Cajun seasoning, salt, and pepper
3. Sprinkle with olive oil
4. Place them on the Air Fryer and cook for 10 minutes
5. Place the fish on each lettuce leaf
6. Garnish with cabbage and carrots

7. Then drizzle with lemon juice on top

8. Serve and enjoy!

Nutritional Contents:

- Calories: 180
- Fat: 7g
- Carbohydrates: 0g
- Protein: 13g

Sockeye Fish

Serving: 4

Prep Time: 5 minutes

Cooking Time: 20 minutes

Ingredients:

- 2-3 fingerling potatoes, thinly sliced
- ½ a bulb fennel, thinly sliced
- 4 tablespoons melted butter
- Salt and pepper to taste
- Fresh dill
- 2 sockeye salmon fillets (6 ounces each)
- 8 cherry tomatoes, halved
- ¼ cup fish stock

Directions:

1. Pre-heat your Air Fryer to 400 degrees F.

2. Take a small-sized saucepan and add salted water, bring the water to a boil.

3. Add potatoes and blanch for 2 minutes.

4. Drain the potatoes and dry them.

5. Cut 2 large-sized rectangles of parchment paper to a sized of 13x15 inches.

6. Add potatoes, melted butter, fennel, fresh ground pepper, and salt to a bowl.

7. Mix the whole mixture well.

8. Divide the veggie mix between the parchment paper pieces.

9. Sprinkle dill on top.

10. Place fillet on top of the veggie piles and season with salt and pepper.

11. Place a cherry tomato on top and drizzle butter.

12. Pour fish stock on top.

13. Fold up the squares and seal them up nicely.

14. Pre-heat your Fryer to 400 degrees Fahrenheit and cook the packets for 10 minutes each.

15. Garnish with a bit of dill and enjoy!

Nutritional Contents:

- Calories: 224
- Fat: 11g
- Carbohydrates: 6g
- Protein: 25g

Crumble Fishcakes

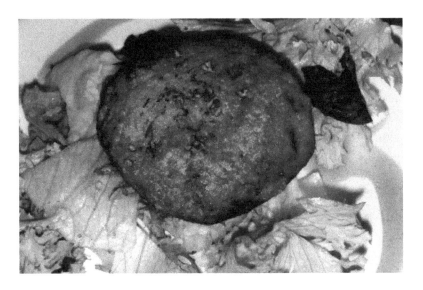

Serving: 4

Prep Time: 5 minutes

Cooking Time: 20 minutes

Ingredients:

- 8 ounces salmon, cooked
- 1 and ½ ounces potatoes, mashed
- 1 small handful capers
- 1 small handful parsley, chopped
- Zest of 1 lemon
- 1 and ¾ ounces plain flour
- Oil spray

Directions:

1. Flake your salmon.

2. Take a bowl and add flaked salmon, zest, dill, capers, mashed potatoes and mix well.

3. Form mixture into small cakes and dust with flour.

4. Chill for 60 minutes.

5. Pre-heat your Air Fryer to 356 degrees F.

6. Cook for 7 minutes until golden.

7. Serve and enjoy!

Nutritional Contents:

- Calories: 210
- Fat: 7g
- Carbohydrates: 25g
- Protein: 10g

Calamari Rings

Serving: 5

Prep Time: 5 minutes

Cooking Time: 15-30 minutes

Ingredients:

- 12 ounces frozen squid
- 1 large egg, beaten
- 1 cup all-purpose flour
- 1 teaspoon ground coriander seeds
- 1 teaspoon cayenne pepper
- ½ teaspoon pepper
- ½ teaspoon salt
- Lemon wedges as needed
- Olive oil for spray

Directions:

1. Take a large-sized bowl and add flour, ground pepper, pepper paprika, salt.

2. Dredge the calamari in the egg and then in the floured mixture.

3. Pre-heat your Air Fryer to 390 degrees F.

4. Place the rings in your Air Fryer basket and cook for 15 minutes until they show a golden brown texture.

5. Cook in batches if needed, garnish with some lemon wedges, and enjoy!

Nutritional Contents:

- Calories: 227
- Fat: 14g
- Carbohydrates: 14g
- Protein: 11g

Baked County Crabs

Serving: 4

Prep Time: 10 minutes

Cooking Time: 15 minutes

Ingredients:

- ½ pound jumbo crab
- Lemon juice to taste
- ¼ cup red onion
- 2 tablespoons parsley, chopped
- Old bay seasoning
- 1 tablespoon basil, chopped
- 3 tablespoons real mayo
- ¼ teaspoon Dijon mustard
- Zest of ½ lemon
- ¼ cup panko breadcrumbs

Directions:

1. Pre-heat your Fryer to 400 degrees F.
2. Mix in real mayo, lemon zest, old bay, and oil in a bowl.
3. Blend the crab meat in a food processor with salt.
4. Transfer processed crab to oil bowl and mix well.
5. Form cakes using the mixture.

6. Dredge the cakes in breadcrumb mix and transfer to Air Fryer.

7. Cook for 15 minutes.

8. Serve with a garnish of basil and parsley.

9. Enjoy!

Nutritional Contents:

- Calories: 126
- Fat: 5g
- Carbohydrates: 1.6g
- Protein: 16g

Greek Mussels

Serving: 4

Prep Time: 25 minutes

Cooking Time: 10 minutes

Ingredients:

- 4 pounds mussels
- Olive oil as needed
- 1 cup white wine
- 2 teaspoons salt
- 2 bay leaves
- 1 tablespoon pepper
- 1 and ½ cup flour
- 1 tablespoon onion powder
- 1 tablespoon fenugreek
- 2 tablespoons vinegar
- 5 garlic cloves
- 4 bread slices
- ½ cup mixed nuts

Directions:

1. Pre-heat your Air Fryer to 350 degrees F.

2. Take your food processor and add garlic, vinegar, salt, nuts, pepper, and crumbs.

3. Process and add olive oil, process again to make a cream.

4. Take pan over medium heat and boil bay leaves in white wine, add mussels and keep simmering until the mussels have opened up.

5. Clean mussels from shells.

6. Add flour to your cream sauce.

7. Cover mussels with the prepared sauce and flour.

8. Transfer mussels to Air Fryer and cook for 10 minutes.

9. Serve with fenugreek and enjoy it!

Nutritional Contents:

- Calories: 100
- Fat: 2g
- Carbohydrates: 18g
- Protein: 10g

Majestic Catfish

Serving: 4

Prep Time: 10 minutes

Cook Time: 20 minutes

Ingredients:

- 4 catfish fillets
- ¼ cup of seasoned fish fry
- 1 tablespoon of olive oil
- 1 tablespoon of chopped parsley

Directions:

1. Pre-heat your Air Fryer to 400 degrees Fahrenheit
2. Take your catfish and rinse it well, pat it dry using a kitchen towel
3. Take a large-sized zip bag and add the fish and seasoning
4. Add a bit of olive oil and coat the fish, shake it well
5. Transfer the fillets to your Fryer and fry for 10 minutes
6. Flip it up and fry for 10 minutes more
7. Flip it for the last time and cook for 1-3 minutes
8. Top it up with parsley and enjoy!

Nutrition Values (Per Serving)

- Calories: 199
- Carbohydrate: 14g
- Protein: 16g
- Fat: 12g

Herbed Up Garlic Lobster Tails

Serving: 3

Prep Time: 15 minutes

Cook Time: 10 minutes

Ingredients:

- 4-ounce lobster tails
- 1 teaspoon garlic, minced
- 1 tablespoon butter
- Salt and pepper to taste
- ½ tablespoon lemon juice

Directions:

1. Take your food processor and add all the ingredients except lobster, blend well.

2. Wash your lobster and halve them using a meat knife.

3. Clean the skin of lobsters.

4. Cover lobsters with marinade.

5. Pre-heat your Fryer t 0380 degree F.

6. Transfer prepared lobster to Air Fryer and bake for 10 minutes.

7. Serve with some fresh herbs and enjoy!

Nutrition Contents:

- Calories: 450
- Fat: 24g
- Carbohydrates: 12g
- Protein: 9g

Tuna Risotto

Serving: 6

Prep Time: 35 minutes

Cooking Time: 10 minutes

Ingredients:

- 1 cup peas 2 (4 ounces) cans tuna, drained
- 4 cups chicken broth, warm
- 1 tablespoon olive oil
- 1 teaspoon black pepper, ground
- 2 cups Arborio rice
- ¼ cup parmesan cheese, grated
- ½ cup yellow onion, minced

Directions:

1. Preheat your Air Fryer to 320 degrees F
2. Season tuna and peas with black pepper
3. Place in the Air Fryer and cook for 10 minutes
4. Heat the oil and add the onion and rice
5. Cook, until it turns into light, brown
6. Add 1 cup warm broth
7. Cook until absorbed and repeat until all the broth is used
8. Stir in the tuna, peas, and parmesan
9. Serve and enjoy!

Nutritional Contents:

- Calories: 553
- Fat: 40g
- Carbohydrates: 23g
- Protein: 52g

Shrimp And Bacon Wraps

Serving: 1

Prep Time: 10 minutes

Cook Time: 10 minutes

Ingredients:

- 1 and a quarter pound of deveined shrimps
- 16 slices of 1 pound thinly sliced bacon

Directions:

1. Take your bacon slices and wrap them up around the shrimp
2. Make sure to start from the bottom and go all way to the top
3. Repeat until all the shrimps are used up
4. Transfer them to your fridge and chill for 20 minutes
5. Preheat your Air Fryer to 390 degrees Fahrenheit
6. Take the shrimp and transfer them to the cooking basket, cook for 5-7 minutes
7. Enjoy!

Nutrition Values (Per Serving)

- Calories: 40
- Carbohydrate: 9g
- Protein: 30g
- Fat: 40g

Herbed Healthy Salmon

Serving: 3

Prep Time: 5 minutes

Cook Time: 16 minutes

Ingredients:

- 2 salmon fillets
- 2 teaspoons garlic, minced
- 1 teaspoon olive oil
- 1 cup white wine vinegar
- 3 tablespoons coconut oil
- Salt as needed
- Dried Italian herbs

Directions:

1. Pre-heat your Air Fryer to 350 degrees Fahrenheit
2. Pat the salmon pieces dry using a kitchen towel and season with salt
3. Transfer them to your Air Fryer and cook for 6 minutes
4. Take a saucepan and add olive oil, heat it over medium heat
5. Add garlic to the pan and stir cook

6. Add white wine vinegar and bring the mix to a boil, cook for 5 minutes
7. Stir in coconut oil and sprinkle Italian herb seasoning
8. Serve the salmon with this sauce
9. Enjoy!

Nutrition Values (Per Serving)

- Calories: 504
- Carbohydrate: 8g
- Protein: 37g
- Fat: 36g

Lovely Garlic Flavored Prawn

Serving: 2

Prep Time: 5 minutes

Cooking Time: 10 minutes

Ingredients:

- 15 fresh prawns
- 1 tablespoon olive oil
- 1 teaspoon chili powder

- 1 tablespoon black pepper
- 1 tablespoon chili sauce, Keto-Friendly
- 1 garlic clove, minced
- Salt as needed

Directions:

1. Pre-heat your Air Fryer to 356 degrees F

2. Wash prawns thoroughly and rinse them

3. Take a mixing bowl and add washed prawn, chili powder, oil, garlic, pepper, chili sauce and stir the mix

4. Transfer prawn to Air Fryer and cook for 8 minutes

5. Serve and enjoy!

Nutritional Contents:

- Calories: 131
- Fat: 10g
- Carbohydrates: 4g
- Protein: 7g

Lemon-Y Garlic Shrimp

Serving: 4

Prep Time: 15 minutes

Cook Time: 8 minutes

Ingredients:

- ¾ pound medium shrimp, peeled and deveined
- 1 and ½ tablespoon fresh lemon juice
- 1 tablespoon olive oil
- 1 teaspoon lemon pepper
- ¼ teaspoon paprika
- ¼ teaspoon garlic powder

Directions:

1. Preheat the Vortex Air Fryer to 400 degrees F and grease an Air fryer basket.

2. Mix lemon juice, olive oil, lemon pepper, paprika, and garlic powder in a large bowl.

3. Stir in the shrimp and toss until well combined.

4. Arrange shrimp into the Air fryer basket in a single layer and cook for about 8 minutes.

5. Dish out the shrimp in serving plates and serve warm.

Nutrition Contents:

- Calories: 200
- Fat: 10g
- Carbohydrates: 2g
- Protein: 23g

Cheesed Up Shrimp

Serving: 4

Prep Time: 20 minutes

Cook Time: 20 minutes

Ingredients:

- 2 tablespoons fresh lemon juice
- Pepper as needed
- ½ teaspoon pepper flakes, crushed
- 1 teaspoon onion powder
- ½ teaspoon dried oregano
- 1 teaspoon dried basil
- 2 tablespoons olive oil
- 4 garlic cloves, minced
- 2 pounds shrimp, peeled and deveined
- 2/3 cup parmesan cheese, grated

Directions:

1. Preheat the Air fryer to 350 o F and grease an Air fryer basket.

2. Mix Parmesan cheese, garlic, olive oil, herbs, and spices in a large bowl.

3. Arrange half of the shrimp into the Air fryer basket in a single layer and cook for about 10 minutes.

4. Dish out the shrimps onto serving plates and drizzle with lemon juice to serve hot.

Nutrition Contents:

- Calories: 386
- Fat: 14g
- Carbohydrates: 5g
- Protein: 57g

Creamy Breaded Shrimp

Serving: 4

Prep Time: 15 minutes

Cook Time: 20 minutes

Ingredients:

- 1 tablespoon Sriracha sauce
- ¼ cup sweet chili sauce
- ½ cup mayonnaise
- 1 pound shrimp, peeled and deveined
- 1 cup panko breadcrumbs
- ¼ cup all-purpose flour

Directions:

1. Preheat the Air fryer to 400 0 F and grease an Air fryer basket.

2. Place flour in a shallow bowl and mix the mayonnaise, chili sauce, and Sriracha sauce in another bowl.

3. Place the breadcrumbs in a third bowl.

4. Coat each shrimp with the flour, dip into mayonnaise mixture and finally, dredge in the breadcrumbs.

5. Arrange half of the coated shrimps into the Air fryer basket and cook for about 10 minutes.

6. Dish out the coated shrimps onto serving plates and repeat with the remaining mixture.

Nutrition Contents:

- Calories: 540
- Fat: 18g
- Carbohydrates: 33g
- Protein: 36g

Coconut Coated Beautiful Shrimp

Serving: 3

Prep Time: 15 minutes

Cook Time: 40 minutes

Ingredients:

- Salt and pepper to taste
- 1 pound large shrimp, peeled and deveined
- ½ cup panko breadcrumbs
- ½ cup sweetened coconut, shredded
- 8 ounces of coconut milk

Directions:

1. Preheat your Vortex Air fryer to 350 0 F and grease an Air fryer basket.

2. Place the coconut milk in a shallow bowl.

3. Mix coconut, breadcrumbs, salt, and black pepper in another bowl.

4. Dip each shrimp into coconut milk and, finally, dredge in the coconut mixture.

5. Arrange half of the shrimps into the Air fryer basket and cook for about 20 minutes.

6. Dish out the shrimps onto serving plates and repeat with the remaining mixture to serve.

Nutrition Contents:

- Calories: 408
- Fat: 23g
- Carbohydrates: 11g
- Protein: 31g

Rice Flour Shrimp

Serving: 3

Prep Time: 20 minutes

Cook Time: 20 minutes

Ingredients:

- 3 tablespoons flour
- 1 pound shrimp, peeled and deveined
- 2 tablespoons olive oil
- 1 teaspoon powdered sugar
- Salt and pepper to taste

Directions:

1. Preheat the Air fryer to 325 0 F and grease an Air fryer basket.

2. Mix rice flour, olive oil, sugar, salt, and black pepper in a bowl.

3. Stir in the shrimp and transfer half of the shrimp to the air fryer basket.

4. Cook for about 10 minutes, flipping once in between.

5. Dish out the mixture onto serving plates and repeat with the remaining mixture.

Nutrition Contents:

- Calories: 299
- Fat: 12g
- Carbohydrates: 11g
- Protein: 35g

Fantastic Prawn Burgers

Serving: 2

Prep Time: 20 minutes

Cook Time: 6 minutes

Ingredients:

- Salt and pepper to taste
- ¼ teaspoon ground turmeric
- ½ teaspoon cumin
- ½ teaspoon red chili powder
- ½ teaspoon garlic, minced
- ½ teaspoon ginger, minced
- 3 cups fresh baby greens
- 2-3 tablespoons onion, chopped
- ½ cup breadcrumbs
- ½ cup prawns, deveined and chopped

Directions:

1. Preheat the Air fryer to 390 0 F and grease an Air fryer basket.

2. Mix the prawns, breadcrumbs, onion, ginger, garlic, and spices in a bowl.

3. Make small-sized patties from the mixture and transfer to the Air fryer basket.

4. Cook for about 6 minutes and dish out in a platter.

5. Serve immediately warm alongside the baby greens.

Nutrition Contents:

- Calories: 240
- Fat: 2g
- Carbohydrates: 37g
- Protein: 18g

Buttery Delicious Scallops

Serving: 3

Prep Time: 15 minutes

Cook Time: 4 minutes

Ingredients:

- ¾ pounds sea scallops, cleaned and patted dry
- Salt and pepper to taste
- ½ tablespoon fresh thyme, minced
- 1 tablespoon butter, melted

Directions:

1. Preheat the Air fryer to 390 o F and grease an Air fryer basket.

2. Mix scallops, butter, thyme, salt, and black pepper in a bowl.

3. Arrange scallops in the Air fryer basket and cook for about 4 minutes.

4. Dish out the scallops in a platter and serve hot.

Nutrition Contents:

- Calories: 202
- Fat: 8g
- Carbohydrates: 4g
- Protein: 28g